esley Andrews 10 MRS Woods N128

esley Andrews 10 MRS Woods N128

Jokes & Riddles

BELL PUBLISHING COMPANY
New York

Copyright © MCMLXXX by Ottenheimer Publishers, Inc.
Library of Congress Catalog Card Number: 80-70007
All rights reserved.
This edition is published by Bell Publishing Company.
A Division of Crown Publishers, Inc.
a b c d e f g h
Published under arrangement with Ottenheimer Publishers, Inc.
Printed in the United States of America.

Tim: Do you like asparagus?

Tom: No, sir! And I'm glad I don't; because if I did, I'd eat it—and I hate the stuff!

Artie: I have a job in a clock factory.
Marty: What do you do?
Artie: Just stand around and make faces.

Why is your nose in the middle of your face?

Because it is the scenter (center).

What does a cat have that no other animal has?

Kittens.

Friend: What is your son going to be when he finishes his education?

Mother: A very, very old man.

Customer: Waiter, I'm late already! Will the pancakes be long?

Waiter: No sir, round!

Tenant: Does the water always come through the roof like this?

Landlord: Oh no, sir. Only when it rains.

Tommy: I didn't think I deserved a zero on this paper!

Teacher: Neither did I, but there weren't any lower marks.

Pop: At your age I could name all the Presidents—and in the proper order.

Son: Yes, but there were only three or four of them then.

Hetty: How long was your last cook with you?

Letty: She was never with us; she was against us from the start.

4

What goes *ha-ha-ha-ha-ha-ha-ha-plop?*
Somebody laughing his head off.

What keeps the moon in place?
Its beams.

What is the best way to grow fat?
Raise pigs.

"Knock-knock.
"Who's there?"
"Zoom."
"Zoom who?"
"Zoom did you expect?"

Sue: Are you trying to make a monkey out of me?
Lou: Why should I take the credit?

"I don't know why they made me come to see you, Doctor," said the little old lady. "Just because I happen to love pancakes."

"I don't see anything wrong with that," said the Doctor. "I love pancakes myself."

"Oh really!" the little old lady shouted and clapped her hands in glee. "Well, you must come over to visit me some day. I've got trunkfuls and trunkfuls of them!"

Grandma: If you wash your face, I'll give you a piece of chocolate. And if you wash behind your ears, I'll give you two pieces.

Petie: Maybe I'd better have a bath!

Three deaf ladies were riding on a bus with the windows wide open. "Goodness, it's windy, isn't it," said the first lady. "No, it's not Wednesday, it's Thursday," said the second lady. "I'm thirsty too," said the third. "Let's all get off the bus and have a cup of tea."

6

Lon: Why did you fall down in the ring? He didn't hit you.

Len: No, but I read his mind.

Susie: My big brother's at Harvard.
Betsy: So's mine.
Susie: What's your brother studying?
Betsy: Nothing. They're studying *him*.

Tim: So this is a battle of wits between you and me, eh?

Tom: No, I never attack a man who's unarmed.

Jimmy: When I got home last night I fell down against the piano.
Jamey: Did you get hurt?
Jimmy: No, I fell on the soft pedal.

The little boy sitting next to the dignified old lady on the bus was sniffling his head off. Finally she turned to him and said, "Little boy, do you have a handkerchief?" "Yes," came the quick reply, "but I don't lend it to strangers."

Butch: What's the difference between a lemon and a head of lettuce?
Buster: I don't know.
Butch: Boy, you'd be a fine one to send after some lemons!

Jimmy's a year and a half old now. And he's been walking since he was eight months!

Really? He must be terribly tired.

Lady Shopper: I don't like the way that whitefish looks.
Fish Man: If you're after looks, why don't you buy a goldfish?

8

What did the cowboy say when he went into his room and saw that his bed was eight feet wide and twenty feet long?

"That's a lot of bunk!"

What colors would you paint the sun and the wind?

The sun rose and the wind blue.

How much money does a skunk have?

One scent.

Diner: Do you serve crabs here?

Waiter: We serve anyone. Sit down!

Customer: A cup of coffee without cream, please.

Waiter: I can't give it to you without cream, but I'll give it to you without milk.

9

Lady: You should be ashamed to be seen begging at my house.

Tramp: Don't feel like that, lady. I've seen a lot worse houses than this one.

What did the boy ghost say to the girl ghost?

"Gee, you're boooo-tiful!"

I am white and tall and thin
(Not a ghost and not a pin)
Through my middle runs a string
And it is a funny thing.
People set my hair alight
So that I will glow at night.
What am I? Draw me here.

Candle.

What did one eye say to the other eye?

Just between us something smells.

"Knock-knock."
"Who's there?"
"Megan."
"Megan who?"
"Megan end to these knock-knock jokes, before I knock-knock you!"

Where do jelly-fish get their jelly?

From the ocean currents.

What is the best way to double a dollar bill?

Fold it.

Bill: How do you spell Mississippi?

Phil: The river or the state?

Which is correct: three and four IS nine or three and four ARE nine?

Neither. Three and four are seven.

If eight sparrows are on a roof and you shoot one, how many are left?

None, the others fly away.

Why does a sick man lose his sense of touch?

Because he doesn't feel well.

Paul: What would you do if you were in my shoes?

Saul: Polish them.

"Knock-knock."
"Who's there?"
"Gladys."
"Gladys who?"
"Gladys summer. Aren't you?"

Poet: Do you think I should put more fire into my poetry?

Publisher: No, I think you ought to put more of your poetry into the fire.

What do ghosts ride at the amusement park?

The roller ghoster.

What do ghosts eat for breakfast?

Ghost Toasties.

What do ghosts call their navy?

The Ghost Guard.

Where can happiness always be found?

In the dictionary.

13

Mechanic: The horn on your car must be broken.
Motorist: No, it's just indifferent.
Mechanic: What do you mean, indifferent?
Motorist: It just doesn't give a hoot.

"Knock-knock."
"Who's there?"
"Dwayne."
"Dwayne who?"
"Dwayne the bathtub—I'm dwowning!"

"Knock-knock."
"Who's there?"
"Amos."
"Amos who?"
"A mosquito bit me. Knock-knock."
"Who's there?"
"Andy."
"Andy who?"
"And he bit me again!"

14

Why did Bob throw the butter out of the window?

To see a butterfly.

She: Hey, how did you get that big gash on your forehead?
He: I bit myself.
She: Come on, how could you bite yourself on the forehead?
He: I stood on a chair.

Customer: How much for the tomatoes?
Grocer: Twenty-five cents a pound.
Customer: Did you raise them yourself?
Grocer: Yes, ma'am! They were only twenty cents yesterday!

Mary opened the refrigerator to get a glass of milk and found a little rabbit curled up on the bottom shelf.

"What are *you* doing there?" asked Mary

"Isn't this refrigerator a Westinghouse?" asked the little rabbit.

"Yes," said Mary, "it is."

"Well," said the rabbit, "I'm just westing."

"My dog knows math. I asked him what 16 minus 16 is and he said nothing."

Why isn't your nose twelve inches long?

Because then it would be a foot.

"Dad, can you help me with my math?"

"Yes, but it wouldn't be right, would it?"

"Probably not!"

What man earns a living by driving his customers away?

A taxi driver.

Inventor: I'm working on a new invention.
Friend: What is it?
Inventor: A perfumed bookmark. If it slips down into the book, you just sniff along the edge until you find your place.

A man came to a doctor with a badly smashed finger. "Doctor," he asked anxiously, "when this heals, will I be able to play the piano?"

"Certainly you will," the doctor promised him.

"You're the best doctor I ever met," said the man happily. "I never could play the piano before."

Milly: I have an idea.

Billy: Beginner's luck!

What did the brownie do with a needle and thread?

Soda cracker.

What did Benjamin Franklin say when he discovered electricity?

"I'm deeply shocked!"

"One of our pigs was sick so I gave him some sugar."

"Why sugar?"

"Haven't you heard of sugar-cured ham?"

Why do you go to bed at night?

Because the bed won't come to you.

"Have you ever seen an apple turnover?"

"No, but I've seen the sugar bowl."

Nell: Will you lend me a dime? I want to call a friend.

Belle: Here's twenty cents. Go call *all* your friends.

Father: Where are you going, Mary?

Mary: I'm going to milk the cow.

Father: What! Not in that pretty hat?

Mary: No, in this pail.

Buster: Did you have a nice vacation?

Brown: No! It rained every single day.

Buster: It couldn't have been that bad. You even have a nice tan.

Brown: That's no tan—it's rust!

What did the lightening bug say when he backed into an electric fan?

I'm de-lighted!

Barry: What part of an automobile kills the most people?

Harry: The nut behind the wheel!

When does a doctor become annoyed?

When he is out of patients.

Teacher: Can you give me an example of wasted energy?

Pupil: Yes, sir—telling a hair-raising story to a bald-headed man.

"Yes, sir," said the captain of the steamboat to a nervous passenger, "I've been running boats on this river for so long that I know where every snag and sandbar is."

Just then, the boat struck a snag and shook from stem to stern. "There!" said the captain. "That's one of them now!"

Cowboy: What kind of saddle do you want—one with a horn or one without?

Dude: Well, there doesn't seem to be too much traffic around here. I guess I won't need the horn.

Teacher: How many sexes are there?
Pupil: Three.
Teacher: Three! Can you name them?
Pupil: Male sex, female sex, and insects.

What does a ghost on guard say when he hears a noise?

"Halt! Who ghosts there?"

What smells most in the zoo?

Your nose.

You have the wrong number.

Then why did you answer if it's the wrong number?

What lies around all night with its tongue hanging out?

A shoe.

Betty: Did you hear about the man who sat up all night trying to figure out where the sun went when it went down?

Olive: No, what happened?

Betty: It finally dawned on him.

Father: Everything is going up! The price of food is up; the price of clothing is up; taxes are up. If only there was one thing that was going down!

Son: This ought to make you feel better, Dad. It's my report card.

Jill: Stop reaching—haven't you got a tongue?

Phil: Yes, but my arms are longer!

What did the adding machine say to the clerk?

"You can count on me!"

Why did the city boy go to the country?

He wanted to see the barn dance.

"Knock-knock."
"Who's there?"
"Oswald."
"Oswald who?"
"Oswald my gum."

22

Diner: This steak is terrible! How was it cooked?
Waiter: Why, it was smothered in onions, sir.
Diner: Well, it sure died hard.

How am I going to divide four potatoes among five people?

Mash 'em!

Tim: Our school has two talking parakeets.

Tom: That's nuthin'.

Tim: Our school has lots of spelling bees!

What color is a ghost?

Boo!

Nat: Is that a real diamond ring?
Matt: If it isn't, I've been cheated out of 29 cents.

How do you catch a squirrel?

Climb up a tree and act like a nut.

Why did Joe throw the clock out the window?

To see time fly.

Jane: How do you like the new English teacher?

Joan: I think she's biased.

Jane: How do you mean?

Joan: Well, she thinks words can be spelled only one way!

What was the snail doing on the superhighway?

About ten inches per hour.

Why is a man's face that is shaved in January like an expensive fur?

Because it's chin-chilly.

What kind of fish do you find in a bird cage?

A perch.

What did the grapes say when the hippo stepped on them?

They didn't say anything, they just let out a little wine.

What's the difference between a hill and a pill?

A hill is hard to get up and a pill is hard to get down.

How can you avoid falling hair?

Jump out of the way.

Polly: People should call you Amazon.
Molly: Why?
Polly: Because you're wide at the mouth.

Why did the golfer wear two pairs of pants?

In case he got a hole in one.

What time is it when the clock strikes thirteen?

Time to fix the clock.

What has five eyes and sleeps in a water bed?

The Mississippi River.

Where do they put old worn-out Volkswagens?

In the Old Volks' Home.

Warden: Boys, this is my tenth year as warden of this prison, and we ought to celebrate the occasion. What kind of party would you suggest?

Voice from the Rear: Open house!

What has four wheels and flies?
A garbage truck.

How was the chowder?

Cold, but not clammy.

How do you know when there's a hyena in the refrigerator?
You can see his footprints in the cheesecake.

How do you get a giraffe out of a cereal box?
Read the directions on the back.

What do you call a baby rifle?
A son of a gun.

"Knock-knock."
"Who's there?"
"Phyllis."
"Phyllis who?"
"Phyllis in on the news."

If a green stone fell into the Red Sea, what would happen?

It would sink.

How do you know when there's a grizzly bear in your bed?

He has the letters "GB" on his pajamas.

Why did the man walk around in polka-dot socks?

He couldn't find his sneakers.

Why did the boy wear green sneakers?

His blue ones were in the laundry.

"Knock-knock."
"Who's there?"
"Jimmy."
"Jimmy who?"
"Jimmy a little kiss!"

If you went to *lepes,* **could you bring back a souvenir?**

Nothing but dreams can come back from sleep.

"Kill all the flies in the house except those from Texas."
"How can I tell which ones are from Texas?"
"Easily, they'll be on the range!"

Boss: Thompson, what are you doing with your feet on the desk?

Thompson: Economy, Sir—my eraser wore out, so I'm using my rubber heels.

What is a man who crosses the ocean twice without taking a bath?

A dirty double crosser.

What is green and jumps three feet every five seconds?

A frog with hiccups.

What do you get if you cross a rhinoceros and a goose?

An animal that honks before it runs you over.

What do geese get when they eat too much cake?

Goose pimples.

Three men were under one umbrella, but none of them got wet. How did they do it?

It wasn't raining.

What could you call the small rivers that flow into the Nile?

Juveniles.

Why does the Statue of Liberty stand in New York harbor?
Because it can't sit down.

What Shakespearean character invented hockey?
Puck.

What kind of geese are found in Portugal?
Portu-geese.

How do you make an elephant stew?
Keep it waiting for two hours.

If you are going on a long hike in the desert, what should you carry?
A thirst-aid kit.

When is a carpenter like a magician?

When he makes a board walk.

Why is a large book like a forest?

It has so many leaves.

Mr. and Mrs. Stingerberry, vacationing in Rome, were being shown through the Colosseum.

"Now, this room," said the guide, "is where the gladiators dressed to fight the lions."

"How does one dress to fight lions?" inquired Mrs. Stingerberry.

"Ve-e-e-e-e-ry slowly," replied the guide.

Teacher: Sally, how many bones do you have in your body?
Sally: 208.
Teacher: Wrong, you only have 207.
Sally: Yes, but I swallowed a chicken bone at lunch.

What do you think of a fellow who works on a hillside?

He's not on the level.

What is the best material for kites?

Fly paper.

Stranger: Boy, will you direct me to the bank?
Boy: I will for a dollar.
Stranger: A dollar! That's high pay, isn't it?
Boy: Sure! Bank directors always get high pay.

I'm still waiting for the turtle soup I ordered.

Well, you know how slow turtles are.

What's as big as an elephant but doesn't weigh anything?

An elephant's shadow.

Why did the man tiptoe past the medicine chest?

He didn't want to wake up the sleeping pills.

Why did the little girl eat bullets?

Because she wanted to grow bangs.

Why was the elephant late in getting on the ark?

He stayed behind to pack his trunk.

What's the use of a snow shovel?

Snow use.

What are the last teeth to appear in the mouth?

False teeth.

34

"How can I stop water from coming into my house?"
"Don't pay the water bill."

"What has four legs, a tail, a trunk and is gray?"
"A mouse going on a trip."

Visitor: And what will you do, dear, when you are as big as your mother?

Little Girl: Diet.

What's easy to get into but hard to get out of?
Trouble.

What color is a guitar?
Plink!

Teacher: Name five things that contain milk.

Jack: Butter, cheese, ice cream, and . . . and two cows.

What's black and white and red all over?

A sunburned penguin.

How did the well-known fruit throw a tantrum in the post office?

A date stamped on a letter.

Why is it difficult for a leopard to hide?

Wherever it goes, it is always spotted.

How did Jonah feel when the whale swallowed him?

Down in the mouth.

Why are people always tired on the first day of April?

Because they've just had a thirty-one-day March.

"What did your mother do when she didn't have enough food to go around?"

"She served square meals."

What did the rhino do when he broke his toe?

He called a toe truck.

Ellen: I'm glad I'm not a mermaid.

Tommy: Why?

Ellen: If I were, I wouldn't have anything to hang up Christmas Eve.

What kind of ears does a train have?

Engineers.

37

A young boy looked up from a magazine he was reading and asked his mother, "What does 'budget' mean? Is it something like a camel?"

His mother, thinking she had misunderstood him, asked him to spell it.

"*B-u-d-g-e-t*," he said, "It says here: 'See Egypt on a budget.'"

What is the last word in airplanes?

Jump!

What has four legs but only one foot?

A bed.

"Why did the moon go to the bank?"

"To change it's quarters."

You probably will not find any paragraph in this book that is as unusual as this paragraph. What is odd about it? That is hard to say, but if you study it, you may catch on. I will add that you might look through thousands of books and paragraphs—all having as many words as this—and not find any that can boast of this oddity. Now, do you know what it is?

The letter "e" is not used.

What did the train engine say when it had a cold?

A-choo, a-choo, a-choo-choo-choo.

What did the mirror do when the boy told it a joke?

It cracked up.

Where did they strike the first nail in the White House?

On the head.

Mother: Now, Willie, you must not be selfish. You must let your brother have the sled half the time.

Willie: But, Mother, I do. I have it going down the hill, and he has it coming up.

Lifeguard: How much weight can you carry?

Bill: A hundred pounds.

Lifeguard: Suppose there was a woman drowning and she weighed two hundred pounds. How would you rescue her?

Bill: I'd make two trips.

Teacher: Mike, give me a sentence using the words defeat, defense, and detail.

Mike: Defeat of de dog went over defense before detail.

As Mark Twain and a friend were coming out of church one morning, it began to rain.

"Do you think it will stop?" asked Twain's friend.

The writer looked at the sky. "It always has," he said.

40

John: Do you believe an apple a day keeps the doctor away?

Mike: I can do better than that: an onion a day keeps *everybody* away!

Why do you always put on your left shoe last?

When you put one on, the other is left.

Why did the boy cut a hole in his umbrella?

So he could see when it stopped raining.

What goes all the way from New York to Los Angeles without moving?

Railroad tracks.

"**What did you get when you crossed a cactus and a porcupine?**"

"Sore hands."

What's the difference between a cloud on a rainy day and a boy who is being spanked?

One pours out rain and the other roars out with pain.

What did Paul Revere say at the end of his famous ride?

Whoa!

A small boy's definition of conscience: Something that makes you tell your mother before your sister does.

What do you call a sculptor who works in the cellar?

A lowdown chiseler.

Operetta—A girl who works for the telephone company.

A seven-year-old girl had gone fishing with her father. After an hour or so, her dad asked, "Are you having any luck?"

"No," she replied. "I don't think the worm is trying."

What's the difference between a bus driver and a bad cold?

One knows the stops, the other stops the nose.

"Knock-knock.
"Who's there?"
"Isabella."
"Isabella who?"
"Isabella ringing? Answer the door!"

Sam: Mom, do you remember that vase that you were always worried I would break?
Mom: Yes, what about it?
Sam: Your worries are over.

Dogcatcher—Spot remover.

One afternoon Tommy came home clutching an expensive new toy.

"Where did you get that?" asked his mother.

"I got it from Johnny for doing him a favor," he said.

"What was the favor?"

"I was hitting him on the head," Tommy explained, "and he said he would give me the toy if I stopped."

Len: You know, my family goes way, way back. Why, my father has Washington's watch.

Ken: That's nothing. My father has Adam's apple.

There were 22 blackbirds sitting on the fence. A farmer shot six of them. How many were left?

None, they all flew away!

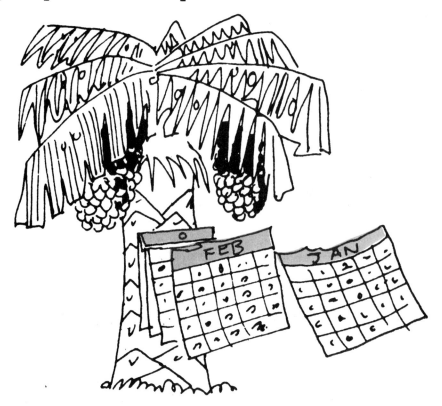

Why is a palm tree like a calendar?

It gives dates.

Bobby: What does *t-e-r-r-i-f-y* spell?

Janie: Terrify.

Bobby: What does *t-i-s-s-u-e* spell?

Janie: Tissue.

Bobby: Now both together, what do they spell?

Janie: Terrify tissue.

Bobby: Heck, no—go ahead!

"Knock-knock.

"Who's there?"

"Marcella."

"Marcella who?"

"Marcella's where I do the washing."

What's gray and looks like gunpowder?

Instant elephant.

Tim: What's worse than a giraffe with a sore throat?

Tom: An elephant with a bloody nose.

A man caught a fish that weighed five pounds plus half of its own weight. How much did it weigh?

Ten pounds.

What pulls without hands, roars without a voice, and bites without a mouth?

The wind.

"Knock-knock.
"Who's there?"
"Noah."
"Noah who?"
"Noah good place to eat around here?"

Teacher: What is a comet?
Student: A star with a tail.
Teacher: Fine. Now name a comet.
Student: Er . . . Lassie.

"Knock-knock."
"Who's there?"
"Banana."
"Banana who?"
"Knock-knock."
"Who's there?"
"Banana."
"Banana who?"
"Knock-knock."
"Who's there?"
"Orange."
"Orange who?"
"Orange you glad I didn't say *banana* again?"

46

Mike: What did you get the little medal for?
Mack: For singing.
Mike: What did you get the big medal for?
Mack: For stopping.

A young lady had just bought a postage stamp. "Must I put it on myself?" she asked.

"Certainly not, Miss," said the postal clerk. "Put it on the letter."

What did Jack Frost say when he proposed to the flower?

"Wilt thou,"—and it wilted.

Why did the camel lie in the road with his feet in the air?

He wanted to trip the birds.

What's brown on the inside and clear on the outside?

A brown bear in a plastic bag.

Why is a grapefruit like a church bell?

It has a peel (peal).

"Knock-knock."
"Who's there?"
"Pecan."
"Pecan who?"
"Pecan somebody your own size."

Why is a baby the least important member of a family?

Because it doesn't count.

Why did the boy jump in the mud and then cross the street twice?

Because he was a dirty double crosser.

What do people in New Zealand do when it snows?

Let it snow.

Waiter—A man who believes money grows on trays.

Bacteria—The rear entrance to a cafeteria.

What did the sea say to the shore?

Nothing. it just waved.

Joe: I broke two wild horses today.

Moe: That's too bad! You'd better be more careful the next time.

City Moron: Why does cream cost more than milk?

Country Moron: Because it's harder for the cows to sit on the small bottles.

What do you get when you cross a centipede with a parrot?

A walkie-talkie.

What man's business is best when things are dullest?

A knife sharpener.

What gives milk and has only one horn?

A milk truck.

"Tell me about geometry."

"When a sapling grew up it said, 'Gee, I'm a tree!' "

Does the sun affect weight?

It makes the daylight.

Why does a chicken cross the road?

For fowl purposes.

Supply Officer: Does the new uniform fit you?

Recruit: The jacket isn't bad, Sir, but the trousers are a little loose around the armpits.

What's red, green, blue and orange?

A plaid tiger.

What did Mrs. Bullet say to Mr. Bullet?

"I'm going to have a BB."

What kind of teeth can you buy for a dollar?

Buck teeth.

What kind of clothing can you make out of banana peels?

Slippers.

Vampire—Somebody who gives you a pain in the neck.

Ray: When I sing, people clap their hands.

Roy: Yeah, clap them over their ears!

When is a little girl's dress like a frog?

When it's a jumper.

What three letters do people hate to write?

I, O, and *U.*

Filing cabinet—A place where you lose things alphabetically.

Two small boys were visiting an art museum. They came upon Rodin's statue of *The Thinker.*

"I wonder what he's thinking about," said one youngster.

"Oh," replied his friend, "he's probably trying to remember where he left his clothes."

Did you hear about the mad scientist who crossed a carrier pigeon with a woodpecker? When the pigeon delivers the message, he can knock on the door.

Which alligators didn't get cavities?

Those that used Crest.

What's green and bumpy, small, and very fast?

A sports pickle.

Meg: Why does your brother sleep in the chandelier?
Greg: Because he's a light sleeper.

"Boy," said Brown to his next-door neighbor Johnson. "What was all the noise over at your house last night?"

"Oh," replied Johnson, "my wife and I had some words. Only I didn't get a chance to use mine."

Gunman: Get ready to die. I'm going to shoot you.
Man: Why?
Gunman: I've always said I'd shoot anyone who looked like me.
Man: Do I look like you?
Gunman: Yes.
Man: Then shoot!

Roy: My dad owns a big yacht.

Ray: It can't be so very big. I heard him say he keeps it in a basin!

Jean: I'm engaged to an Irishman.
Joan: Oh, really?
Jean: No, O'Reilly.

Jones: "Have any luck hunting lions in Africa?"

Smith: "Yes, I didn't meet any!"

The embarrassed city hostess said to her country cousin, "I thought I suggested you come after supper."

"Right," said the country cousin. "That *is* what I came after."

What is the quietest game in the world?

Bowling. You can hear a pin drop.

Did you have a good time on your vacation?

Yes.   What did you do?

We had a good time.

Ask a silly question and you get a silly answer!

Johnny: (offering some candy) Here, honey, sweets to the sweet!

Mary: Oh, thank you, and won't you have some of these nuts?

What is a sure sign of an early spring?

A cat with her back arched, watching a hole in the wall.

Then there was the tenderfoot, camping out overnight for the first time, who asked the scoutmaster, "Pardon me, sir, but where do I plug in my toothbrush?"

Visitor: Is this a healthy place?
Native: It sure is. When I came here, I couldn't utter a word. I had scarcely a hair on my head. I was too weak to walk across the room. Why, I had to be lifted from my bed!
Visitor: That's amazing. How long have you been here?
Native: I was born here.

Salesman: These are especially strong shirts, madam. They simply laugh at the laundry.

Customer: I know. The last bunch you sold me came back with their sides split.

Six-year-old trying to thread a needle: "Come on, now, say 'ahhhh!'"

Joe: Who did you marry?
Moe: A woman.
Joe: Did you ever hear of anyone who didn't marry a woman?
Moe: Yes, my sister.

When is a door not a door?

When it's ajar.

Why does a hen lay an egg?

Because she can't lay a brick.

Doctor: What do you dream about at night?
Dopey: Baseball.
Doctor: Don't you dream about anything else?
Dopey: No, just about baseball, night after night.
Doctor: Don't you ever dream about food?
Dopey: What? And miss my turn at bat?

A furrier tried to invent a new fur by crossing a mink with a gorilla. It didn't work, though—the sleeves were too long.

What is the difference between a mouse and a beauty queen?

One charms the hes while the other harms the cheese.

What is the difference between sea surf and a baby?

One rolls upon the shore, and the other rolls upon the floor.

A small boy was standing near an escalator in a department store, watching the moving handrail.

"Is there anything wrong?" asked a saleslady.

"Nope," he said, "I'm just waiting for my gum to come around again."

58

Doctor: I don't like the looks of your husband.
Wife: I don't either, but he is good to the children.

Jay: Is he a real indian?

Ray: Yes.

Jay: But I thought indians always wore feathers!

Ray: It must be the moulting season.

Mike: Do you know my parents?
Ike: No, I don't.
Mike: (Holding out his hand) Meet my paw.

Don: That candy you're eating looks good.
Dan: It is good.
Don: It makes my mouth water.
Dan: To show you what a good guy I am, here's a blotter!

What did the rug say to the floor?

Don't move. I have you covered.

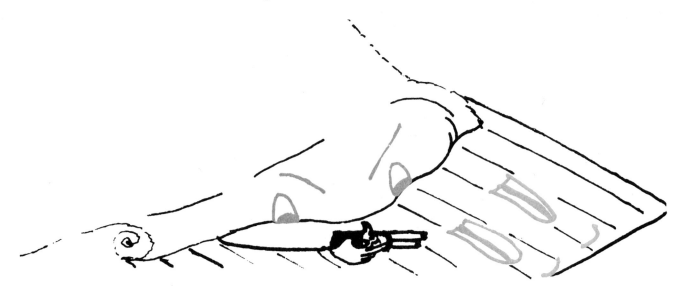

Which dog has more legs, one dog or no dog?

No dog has more legs, because no dog has five legs.

Iron Age—The period before permanent press.

Don: I wonder why a hummingbird hums?!

Dan: I guess he doesn't know the words.

Pit: Can you carry a tune?

Pat: Certainly!

Pit: Well, carry the one you just finished out to the yard and bury it!

What has hands but no feet, a face but no eyes, tells but does not talk?

A clock.

Who is larger — Mr. Larger or Mr. Larger's baby?

Mr. Larger's baby, because he's a little Larger.

Shopper—Someone who likes to go buy-buy.

How do you keep fish from smelling?

Cut off their noses.

Salesman: This hair tonic will grow hair on a golf ball!

Customer: Who wants hair on a golf ball?

Mel: If bananas come under fruit and carrots come under vegetables, what does an egg come under?

Nell: I don't know. What does an egg come under?

Mel: A chicken.

What time of day was Adam created?

Just a little before Eve.

What comes after the letter 'A'?

All of the other letters.

Forger—A man who's always ready to write a wrong.

Helen: I don't like this photograph. It doesn't do me justice.

Ellen: You don't want justice—you want mercy!

Al: Do you know what a satellite is?

Hal: Sure, it's what you put on your horse if you're going to ride him after dark.

Why are artists so careful to sign their pictures?

So that people can tell the top from the bottom.

When are boys like bears?

When they are bare-(bear-) footed.

Minnehaha—Small laugh.

Judge: Now tell me, why did you steal that purse?

Prisoner: Your Honor, I wasn't feeling well, and I thought the change would do me good.

Mrs. Brown: My daughter has arranged a little piece for the piano.

Next-Door Neighbor: Fine! It's about time we had a little peace.

Ed: This is a perfect spot for a picnic.

Ted: It must be. Fifty million ants can't be wrong!

Why is your heart like a policeman?

Because it follows a regular beat.

What do you get if you blow your hair dryer down a rabbit hole?

Hot cross bunnies.

64